T0157691

OPPOSITION
GIVES YOU AN
OPPORTUNITY

BOBBIE WILLIAMS

Order this book online at www.trafford.com
or email orders@trafford.com

Most Trafford titles are also available at major online book retailers.

Printed in the United States of America.

ISBN: 978-1-4669-1680-7 (sc)
ISBN: 978-1-4669-1682-1 (hc)
ISBN: 978-1-4669-1681-4 (e)

Library of Congress Control Number: 2012903179

Trafford rev. 04/12/2012

 www.trafford.com

North America & international
toll-free: 1 888 232 4444 (USA & Canada)
phone: 250 383 6864 ♦ fax: 812 355 4082

CONTENTS

Thank you God, for allowing me to write my first book.

To encourage those that are doing a great work and it appears nothing is happening. It may seem like nothing is happening but you've got to know that God is working on your behalf. You should have no doubt about your assignment.

God allowed me to write this book to encourage myself. He has done and is doing what He promised in my personal life. Just as I heard every prophetic word about ministry, I keep working and praying for God to send people with a mind work. I must continue to believe in my heart that I'm doing a great work. Regardless of oppositions of all types, if anybody is going to quit, **let the devil quit**!

Oppositions have given me opportunities that God's glory has been revealed in my life. Because I have not given up, because I have not quit, because I have not thrown in the towel, I have given **my eyes a chance to see** His promises fulfilled in my life. I must continue to see the fulfillment of ministry as well. It's not always easy but I do know it is well worth it. Be encouraged!

To God be the glory! Praise and honor for what He has done in the past, for what He's doing right now and for what He's going to do!

Opposition

1. the act of opposing.
2. an opposed condition; resistance, contradiction, contrast, hostility, etc.

Opportunity knocks: The door of opportunity is open, a phrase that has been coined and is generally used for one to make some type of investment or decision when conditions are favorable. It is seldom viewed when conditions are less favorable to view opposition as an opportunity. We want our desires, ambitions and goals given to us on a silver platter. No strains, no struggles, no stress, no mess, and especially no work on our part. When the door of opportunity is open, we want to merely just walk in. Some are fortunate to be born with a silver spoon in their mouth. In Christ we were all born the same: born-again. Once sinners, now saved, it qualifies us to desire and obtain the things of God through consistency and perseverance. The oppositions we face can enrich us in ways we can never imagine. Paul, a sinner was on the road of destruction to destroy. He is now born again, preaching and striving for the very thing he once kicked against.

Apostle Paul comes to mind, when the winds of opposition blew the ship apart (Acts chapters 27 & 28 KJV). In the midst of the destruction Paul was able to make it on broken pieces. The same pieces that were once bonded together that contained him as a prisoner, were the same pieces once broken by the storm that supported him as the tide brought him current—his current opportunity. The opportunity to witness! The opportunity to heal! The Bible clearly lets us know that afflictions with come. Many *are* the afflictions (stresses, hurt, wounds, strife, discouragement, grief, burdens, of the righteous: but the Lord delivereth him out of them all. Psalms 34:19 (KJV).

When God is with us and is the controlling factor on the ship of life we too can make it on broken pieces. God keeps us together when the storms of life carry us through rough seasons. If the devil had known, he would've left you alone! But as for you, ye thought evil against me; *but* God meant it unto good, to bring to pass, as *it is* this day, to save much people alive (Gen 50:20 KJV). Your oppositions give you the opportunity to share your faith with others. Not only to share your faith but to be positive about what you know. Many are waiting for opportunities to witness to others. Believe it or not, the oppositions you have faced in life have already given you an opportunity to become a witness of God's glory. If you have been opposed with sickness and God has healed you, *that's your opportunity*. If you have been opposed with unemployment and God has made a way for you, *that's your opportunity*. If you've been opposed with any type of addiction and now you're clean, *that's your opportunity*. If you've been opposed with brokenness and divorce, and God has healed you and re-established your joy, *that's your opportunity*. Many people feel like they're alone, but they're not. You've gone through it. You have the authority because you've experienced it. Tell your story and you'll see that opposition has a way of uniting people. Someone will be able to identify with you in a situation they're facing. Opportunity is knocking at your door. Do you hear it? How will you answer it?

Many flee opposition to only end up in a worser state. You've got to learn to stay on board. Paul faced the opposition, he had heard from God, except these abide in the ship, ye cannot be saved (Acts 27:31). There was a storm in my life. My life as I knew it is was broken apart. I distinctly heard God say "Bobbie Jean don't look at the storm". The hymnist Ruth Caye Jones best writes it like this: In times like these we need a Savior. In times like these we need in anchor. So you be sure, be very sure that your anchor holds and grips the Solid Rock. That Rock is Jesus, he is the one. That Rock is Jesus, he's the only one. So you be sure, be very sure that your ankle holds and grips the Solid Rock. It is very important that you hear God during opposing times. Your life depends on it.

When faced with opposition, instead of complaining wouldn't it be great to say? "God, You get the Glory out of my life". I'm reminded of a song by recording artist Earnest Pugh, the lyrics are: I need your glory, I want your glory. Less of me and more of you is what I need. Upon reading this book I pray that you will no longer view opposition as inopportune.

Op*position* gives you an opport*unity*

Allow opposition to change your position, and give you an opportunity to come together in unity to do a great work!

Prayer shows us the work to be done. Prayer invokes us to work. When we're working towards something we will pray. No prayer causes us to neglect work. A lot of us aren't working because we aren't praying.

CHAPTER 1

Prayer Answered

Nehemiah wanted to know about the Jews that had escaped captivity. He wanted to know the condition of Jerusalem. There are people that are genuinely concerned about your welfare and then there are those that just want to know of your plight or your downfall. When inquiries are made about someone, carefully discern if it's genuine. If you don't discern the spirit behind the inquiry you will deliver news to the enemy of the person sought after. <u>Discerning is seeing what is not obvious.</u>

In the Scriptures you will find the situation that has occurred concerning the Jews:

> *The words of Nehemiah the son of Hachaliah. And it came to pass in the month Chisleu, in the twentieth year, as I was in Shushan the palace, 2 That Hanani, one of my brethren, came, he and certain men of Judah; and I asked them concerning the Jews that had escaped, which were left of the captivity, and concerning Jerusalem. 3 And they said unto me, The*

1

remnant that are left of the captivity there in the province are in great affliction and reproach: the wall of Jerusalem also is broken down, and the gates thereof are burned with fire. *4* And it came to pass, when I heard these words, that I sat down and wept, and mourned certain days, and fasted, and prayed before the God of heaven, *5* And said, I beseech thee, O LORD God of heaven, the great and terrible God, that keepeth covenant and mercy for them that love him and observe his commandments: *6* Let thine ear now be attentive, and thine eyes open, that thou mayest hear the prayer of thy servant, which I pray before thee now, day and night, for the children of Israel thy servants, and confess the sins of the children of Israel, which we have sinned against thee: both I and my father's house have sinned. *7* We have dealt very corruptly against thee, and have not kept the commandments, nor the statutes, nor the judgments, which thou commandedst thy servant Moses. *8* Remember, I beseech thee, the word that thou commandedst thy servant Moses, saying, If ye transgress, I will scatter you abroad among the nations: *9* But if ye turn unto me, and keep my commandments, and do them; though there were of you cast out unto the uttermost part of the heaven, yet will I gather them from thence, and will bring them unto the place that I have chosen to set my name there. *10* Now these are thy servants and thy people, whom thou hast redeemed by thy great power, and by thy strong hand. *11* O Lord, I beseech thee, let now thine ear be attentive to the prayer of thy servant, and to the prayer of thy servants, who desire to fear thy name:

and prosper, I pray thee, thy servant this day, and grant him mercy in the sight of this man. For I was the king's cupbearer. Neh 1:1-11 (KJV)

In response to Nehemiah's inquiry, he's told of the great afflictions and reproach. Many will find themselves in the same state as the remnant Jews, you've escaped captivity, but all is not well. It must be understood that there will be afflictions whether you are bound or free. Afflictions are not always physical. It doesn't always mean sickness. Anything that bothers you, causes you distress, pain, trouble and suffering is an affliction. (Many *are* the afflictions of the righteous: but the LORD delivereth him out of them all.) Psalms 34:19 (KJV) Your neighbor, your husband, your wife, your father, your mother, your children, your co-worker can cause afflictions in your life. Your affliction may be people that are in church that oppose your assignment from God.

The wall that protected the remnant Jews and kept the enemy out had to be built and strengthened. When the very thing that protects you is broken, look for the enemy to gain entry. When the enemy tries to come, start building. *(But ye, beloved, building up yourselves on your most holy faith, praying in the Holy Ghost,) Jude 1:20 (KJV)* Began to speak the Word of God, it builds a wall that will keep the enemy out. (. . . *When the enemy shall come in like a flood, the Spirit of the LORD shall lift up a standard against him.) Isaiah 59:19 (KJV)* Just as the devil challenged God to move Job's hedge of protection, the devil fights daily to find a *breach* concerning us. God gave the devil limited permission against

---

* breach-(noun) 1: infraction or violation of law, obligation, tie, or standard; 2 a: a broken, ruptured, or torn condition or area; b: a gap (as in a wall) made by battering;

Job. The access the devil had to Job opened the door to afflictions and reproach. In your walk with God you may find your hedge of protection removed for a season. That season will last as long as God allows. During this season of struggles, trials and testing, allow these oppositions to give you an opportunity that God's glory would be revealed. Nehemiah faced opposition from the people of the land. He had strong personal faith and confidence in divine guidance and help.

The wall of Jerusalem had great political, social, and religious significance for the people of Judah. Israel's enemies knew that if the wall was rebuilt, the Jews would gain political power, security, self-determination and so they opposed the rebuilding of the wall fiercely. The walls of Jerusalem were built gradually. So it is with the Word of God, you build up the Word of God gradually in your life. You're not going to become an overnight success. (*Study to shew thyself approved unto God, a workman that needeth not to be ashamed, rightly dividing the word of truth.*) 2 Tim 2:15 (KJV) It takes time to build your spiritual wall with the Word of God. We get discouraged because we feel like the word doesn't work. If you feel like the word doesn't work. If you feel like your wall isn't strong enough. Don't tear it down, don't walk off, don't leave it hanging, go back to the foundation and keep building. Keep working. Nehemiah and his workers had to go and complete what had been neglected and left incomplete. Be sure you have a foundation to build upon. (*And I say also unto thee, That thou art Peter, and upon this rock I will build my church; and the gates of hell shall not prevail against it.*) Matt 16:18 (KJV) God will send you a Nehemiah that has heard of your plight and he will help you reach completion. The Temple was finished but the wall was broken down and the gates were burned. When Jesus Christ saved us, He did a finished work. It is up to us to protect what we have.

(What? know ye not that your body is the temple of the Holy Ghost which is in you, which ye have of God, and ye are not your own? **20** *For ye are bought with a price: therefore glorify God in your body, and in your spirit, which are God's.) 1 Cor 6:19-20 (KJV)*

The work was long neglected until Nehemiah arrived to complete it. There's a lot of work that's neglected. When the wall is broken down in our lives and the gates get burned we have too many excuses not to work during our brokenness. With broken down walls and burned gates work is still required by God. We have a tendency to prolong our stay in our afflictions. You have got to keep working. Just because you're going through don't stop working. There are times that afflictions will cause you to stop talking, stop confessing, and stop doing the things you used to do for God. You slack up in your church attendance. There are times during you affliction that you will cease from reading. You will cease from studying. It's the same as being sick, you may not eat for three days, you may not get out of bed for a week, but eventually you've got to get back up. Yes, your afflictions will come but don't let your afflictions overtake you and cause you to become an invalent in the spirit. Don't let your afflictions cripple you when it's not a life-crippling disorder. Don't get crippled when it's not a life-crippling situation. You look around at your surroundings. You may want to quit. You may feel it's too much to attempt. You may see your situation as a giant when it's really a grasshopper situation. You may not even know where to begin the building process. You know the work needs to be done. Today becomes tomorrow. Tomorrow becomes next week. Next week becomes next month. Next month because next year. Each year begins to pass and the work has long been neglected. Nehemiah will tell you, you neglected the work but I'm here because God sent me to help you start the building process. Nehemiah knew his purpose and whatever the affliction, whatever was going on, he was sent to do a work.

Nehemiah was greatly affected by the bad news he heard. He weeps, mourns certain days, fasted and prayed before God. Bad news will cause leaders to feel burdened. How many of us are weeping, fasting and praying before God because of the situation we're in? Why do we always expect the leaders/pastors to do the weeping? Why do we expect the leaders/pastors to do all the praying? Why do we expect them to turn down their plates? Why don't we as born-again believers get the heart of leadership? The heart of the ministry and say, I don't like what's going on; therefore I need to seek God in prayer. Everyone expects the leaders/pastors to do it all. Nehemiah didn't build the walls and hang the gates by himself. He had help.

Nehemiah goes to God in prayer knowing that He is a covenant keeping God. Asking for God's undivided attention *(v6 Let thine ear now be attentive, and thine eyes open, that thou mayest hear the prayer of thy servant, which I pray before thee now, day and night, for the children of Israel thy servants, and confess the sins of the children of Israel, which we have sinned against thee: both I and my father's house have sinned.)* He began confessing the sins of the children of Israel, his sins and the sins of his father's house. Nehemiah prays to God for everyone. His prayer includes confession, repentance, mercy, and favour.

Nehemiah is aware of his duties in the king's house, but he is more aware of his need to do the KING'S work. Nehemiah was sad but continued serving King Artaxerxes. Isn't it funny how we say God has called us to do something but we neglect our other duties? God gives assignments to those that he knows will work and remain faithful in the natural things. Nehemiah was sad but he didn't quit his job. Nehemiah knew that being a servant to the king, there was a certain countenance that you maintained. It was the first time he was ever sad in the king's presence. No doubt he tried to keep his sadness outside the presence of the king. Nehemiah didn't want to be a distraction, but the news was so heavy on him. He could no longer hide his feelings from the king. The situation with the Jews was not a trivial matter. Nehemiah was afraid to come into the king's presence with a sad countenance. King Artaxerxes saw something was wrong. This was not the usual appearance for his cupbearer. The king wants to know. You're not sick but something is wrong.

Persian kings were very exacting in their demand concerning their servants. The ruler could have a servant executed for breach of court etiquette. Servants dressed a certain way, a certain style. There was a proper way to handle yourself when you served the king. What about situations in your life? How do we come before the KING (*Our Heavenly Father/the King of kings)?* How do we come before the leaders/pastors? When leaders/pastors ask for church etiquette during servitude some members complain," that's just too much," "can we make our own decision?" There are certain ways that show you are a servant in the house of the king. We identify people by the way they dress and how they handle themselves in the king's house. People want to do what they want. You don't want to be out a distraction in the house of Lord. Surely you don't want to be out of order. You want to be a good servant. There were certain things a servant had to do. Anything out of order, including his countenance, if the servant knew he was going before the king, he knew he'd better get himself together. Nehemiah had reverential fear of the king. Do we have reverential fear of the King of kings? How do we enter into His presence? Just as Nehemiah, when you've served your best, God will work in your favour.

At hearing Nehemiah's reason and request King Artaxerxes gave him permission to take a leave of absence from his natural work to do God's work *(because of prayer)*. Are you willing to take time off your job to do God's work when you see the great need of building walls that can help end afflictions and reproach? Do you feel the need to get to the place where God has assigned you to help the ministry? God is a God of order. Too many of us want our prayers answered but we have no reverence or respect for the authority over us (the leaders/pastors). You think you've heard from God, you quit serving and leave without a word. Again I reiterate, God is a God of order.

Knowing that he had the king's favor, and knowing what THE KING had put in his heart, Nehemiah set a time for his return. Favor provided the resources needed to do the work. When God gives you a work to do or a vision He will provide provisions for the vision. When God puts something in your heart, His cause is to make it happen. God uses ordinary people. He deals with the heart of man. We are His hands, His feet, His eyes, His ears. God uses resources that have already been prepared to meet needs. That's why it is so important to listen for the voice of God. You may be the answer to someone's prayer. There will be times you will start out with nothing but a prayer. That's where faith comes in, to believe that God is going to provide. We're still trying to look out of our fleshly 20/20 vision to see how the assignment is going to be done. When Nehemiah began to pray to God he didn't know how he was going to build the wall. He didn't know how he was going to get the gates hung. He didn't even know if he could get a leave of absence. But he prayed and God answered his prayer. Did God give you an assignment? Did He give you a vision? Are you still reasoning in your mind how it's going to be done? Have you prayed about it? Start praying and trust God to make happen what you can't.

REFLECTION QUESTIONS

1. During your walk with God, have you been led by the Spirit to carry out or complete an assignment? What was your first response?
2. Have you faced oppositions because of ministry work that was neglected and you felt burdened to complete the task?
3. How did you handle the opposition from within the church walls?
4. Have you ever started an assignment with nothing and it became more overwhelming than you expected?

PRAYER

Father, Help me to be obedient to the call on my life. Whatever the assignment you have assigned to me, help me to be prayerful and faithful to your direction. Strengthen me in times of opposition. Help me to complete what you have charged to my hands, that You may be glorified. Amen.

CHAPTER 2

The Provocation of Opposition

Then I came to the governors beyond the river, and gave them the king's letters. Now the king had sent captains of the army and horsemen with me. **10** *When Sanballat the Horonite, and Tobiah the servant, the Ammonite, heard of it, it grieved them exceedingly that there was come a man to seek the welfare of the children of Israel.* **11** *So I came to Jerusalem, and was there three days.* **12** *And I arose in the night, I and some few men with me; neither told I any man what my God had put in my heart to do at Jerusalem: neither was there any beast with me, save the beast that I rode upon.* **13** *And I went out by night by the gate of the valley, even before the dragon well, and to the dung port, and viewed the walls of Jerusalem, which were broken down, and the gates thereof were consumed with fire.* **14** *Then I went on to the gate of the fountain, and to the king's pool: but there was no place for the beast that was under me to pass.* **15** *Then went I up in the* *night by the brook, and viewed the wall, and turned back, and entered by the gate of the valley, and so returned. 16 And the rulers knew not whither I went, or what I did; neither had I as yet told it to the Jews, nor to the priests, nor to the nobles, nor to the rulers, nor to the rest that did the work. 17 Then said I unto them, Ye see the distress that we are in, how Jerusalem lieth waste, and the gates thereof are burned with fire: come, and let us build up the wall of Jerusalem, that we be no more a reproach. 18 Then I told them of the hand of my God which was good upon me; as also the king's words that he had spoken unto me. And they said, Let us rise up and build. So they strengthened their hands for this good work. 19 But when Sanballat the Horonite, and Tobiah the servant, the Ammonite, and Geshem the Arabian, heard it, they laughed us to scorn, and despised us, and said, What is this thing that ye do? will ye rebel against the king? 20 Then answered I them, and said unto them, The God of heaven, he will prosper us; therefore we his servants will arise and build: but ye have no portion, nor right, nor memorial, in Jerusalem. Neh 2:9-20 (KJV)*

Sanballat and Tobiah were enemies of the Jews. They were grieved because someone came to seek the welfare of the children of Israel. Your enemy is not going to be happy about you rebuilding your life. Nehemiah has three days of rest from his journey. Being properly rested before we begin God's work is very important. When properly rested we will see and think clearly. We will be at our best. We will be more perceptive. You will not be able to see what God wants you to see when you're tired. After Elijah had went a days journey into the wilderness the Angel of the Lord touched Elijah and told him to "arise and eat the journey is great." When we're tired we see grasshoppers as GIANTS. Many of us do not see rest as a factor when it comes to serving God. We have a tendency to prioritize menial things and do all else that satisfies us and others, when the time arrives for us to work for God we are too tired and unprepared. Worn out, how can we help others? How can we attend to the things of God? How can we build ministry? Nehemiah knew he had a great work to do, therefore he rested. After being in Jerusalem three days Nehemiah gets up in the night to do an inspection tour. He took a few men with him but didn't reveal to them what God had put in his heart. I believe that our omniscient God lead Nehemiah out at night and didn't allow him to tell anyone about his purpose because Nehemiah probably was closely watched during the night and the news of his inspection tour would have gotten back to Sanballat-*(the enemy is secret)*. The enemy of the Jews had already heard that help was on the way.

Be aware that you have secret enemies. These are the ones that act as if they're happy for you but aren't. These will be the ones that ask to help only to sabotage the assignment. It would be interesting to know how many secret enemies you have around. *(When the wicked, even mine enemies and my foes, came upon me to eat up my flesh, they stumbled and fell. 3 Though an host should encamp against me, my heart shall not fear: though war should rise against me, in this will I be confident.) Psalms 27:2-3 (KJV)* Some of your assignments didn't reach completion because you had secret enemies around you and you shared too much information with the enemy. Who is my neighbor, better yet who is my enemy? Your family could be your enemy. Your parents might be your enemy.

Sad to say, some of the people in your church could very well be your enemy: your secret enemy. Nehemiah came to Jerusalem. Sanballat opposed Nehemiah in the building of the city wall of Jerusalem and seeking the welfare of the children of Jerusalem. When you have work to do for the Lord you will be opposed. Just know that before you reach your place of assignment opposition is already there.

After Nehemiah got the few men to the work site they saw for themselves the distress the Jews were in. These few said; let's do something about the situation so there will be no more reproach. *(For with God nothing shall be impossible.) Luke 1:37 (KJV)* After their spirit agreed with Nehemiah's task, he now reveals to them about the hand of God which was good upon him. He told them of the king's approval. They agreed to build. They strengthened their hands for this good work. *(I can do all things through Christ which strengtheneth me.) Phil 4:13 (KJV)* Only a few to do a great work will cause the enemy to ridicule you, laugh in your face and question your assignment. Sanballat, Tobiah, and Geshem despised Nehemiah and the few men for having the nerve to attempt to rectify the situation of Jerusalem and the remnant Jews. They laugh them to *scorn. You've taken an inspection tour and made a decision to start working on your broken down condition. The enemy is laughing at your situation. He thinks you're a big joke when you say you're going to do something about it. He thinks it's a joke when you say you're going to have certain things

---

* scorn-(noun) open contempt or disdain. (verb) 1. Express scorn for. 2. reject in a contemptuous way. contempt (noun) the feeling that a person or a thing is worthless or beneath consideration. disdain (noun) the feeling that someone or something is unworthy of one's consideration or respect.

in life and cause things to happen. Just keep working while your enemies are laughing. You will get immune to the laughter. God will condition you to prayerfully take it like a child of God. When Nehemiah went to build the wall and the gates the enemy thought it was impossible. He was going to attempt to do what no one else had. In spite of laughter Nehemiah proclaims that God will prosper the work. There are some seemingly impossible situations in life that will cause people to laugh at us. Has anyone laughed you to scorn lately for believing God? Has this type of opposition given you an opportunity? *(Whatsoever thy hand findeth to do, do it with thy might; . . .) Eccl 9:10 (KJV)* In spite of <u>opposition</u> the work begins from a <u>position</u> of <u>unity</u>.

> *Then Eliashib the high priest rose up with his brethren the priests, and they builded the sheep gate; they sanctified it, and set up the doors of it; even unto the tower of Meah they sanctified it, unto the tower of Hananeel. 2 And next unto him builded the men of Jericho. And next to them builded Zaccur the son of Imri.*
>
> *3 But the fish gate did the sons of Hassenaah build, who also laid the beams thereof, and set up the doors thereof, the locks thereof, and the bars thereof. Neh 3:1-3 (KJV)*

They built the sheep gate first, sanctified it and set it apart. This gate held the sacrifices. We try to do other things first when we should put first things first. The sheep gate (the heart) where our lives become a living sacrifice. What's most important? (*I beseech you therefore, brethren, by the mercies of God, that ye present your bodies a living sacrifice, holy, acceptable unto God, which is your reasonable service). Romans 12:1 (KJV)* Repairing our heart for sacred use. Guard the gateway to your heart (your spirit). They worked on the sheep gate to protect the sanctified sheep. Guard the entrance (gateway) to your heart to keep the devil out. If you don't sanctify and guard the gateway to your heart the purity of your heart can become contaminated, becoming useless for God's use. When your heart has not been sanctified and the gates not properly hung the enemy can gain access. *(What? know ye not that your body is the temple of the Holy Ghost which is in you, which ye have of God, . . .) 1 Cor 6:19 (KJV)*

They laid the locks. The crossbars held the gate shut from within the walls. Anyone couldn't just come and pull the doors open from the outside. The gate has to be opened from the inside. People can be antagonistic and sarcastic, but it is up to you in all things. No matter what's done it's up to you from the inside. You must discipline yourself not to react in response to others actions. The fish gate was built after the sheep gate. The sheep gate held the sacrifices. The fish gate was where the resources were. The fish being a financial resource was marketed and brought in part of the people's wealth. Our wealth is on the inside and we use should not open it up and allow the enemy to come in and take our resources. *(For God, who commanded the light to shine out of darkness, hath shined in our hearts, to give the light of the knowledge of the glory of God in the face of Jesus Christ. 7 But we have this treasure in earthen vessels, that the excellency of the power may be of God, and not of us.) 2 Cor 4:6-7 (KJV)* What's going to make you survive? What's going to get you over to the next month? What's going to cause you to live? Let the enemy know he's not going to come in and take your stuff. You say this with authority: "The Devil is a Lie." If the enemy gains entry you will be the one to open the gate from the INSIDE! It's up to you. The Word of God says guard your spiritual treasure with all diligence. You've got to protect (secure) your heart. Make up your mind you're going to keep this treasure and you cannot allow robbers to take what you have. You cannot allow people to steal your joy and take your peace. The enemy can try to break your doors down. You are not going to let him in. The enemy can say all kinds of things, character assassination, misrepresentation, bad influence, but one thing you cannot allow him to do, is to get in your heart. The fish gate locked from the inside. Bars refer to hooks or catches holding the crossbars at each end. You've got to hook the gateway to your heart. Get rooted and grounded in the Word of God. Hook yourself in the Word of God so that it will be the hooks that hold you fast and stop depending on your own inabilities. God doesn't save or keep your flesh. He keeps the active word that is in your heart. GUARD THE WORD! *(Thy word have I hid in mine heart, that I might not sin against thee.) Psalms 119:11 (KJV)*

The high priests, priests, goldsmiths, apothecaries, rulers, the men and women, all working together to build the gates and walls. Everyone working next unto each other. *(For ye are all the children of God by faith in Christ Jesus. 27 For as many of you as have been baptized into Christ have put on Christ. 28 There is neither Jew nor Greek, there is neither bond nor free, there is neither male nor female: for ye are all one in Christ Jesus.) Gal 3:26-28* (KJV) The purpose was to complete the repairs as soon as possible. Team work. **T**ogether **E**ffectively **A**chieving **M**ore! Different genders, different status, and different occupations. Team work. **T**ogether **E**veryone **A**ccomplishing **M**ore! In our churches you will find different genders, different status, different occupations and different gifts. These differences shouldn't hinder us from building and repairing the House of God. **4** *(Now there are diversities of gifts, but the same Spirit. **5** And there are differences of administrations, but the same Lord. **6** And there are diversities of operations, but it is the same God which worketh all in all.) 1 Cor 12:4-6 (KJV)* If brethren and sisters in the Lord would work together in our churches we would begin to see a great work accomplished. *(And if a house be divided against itself, that house cannot stand.) Mark 3:25 (KJV)* Let's make a TEAM effort to build the Kingdom of God. A spirit of unity will bring a spirit of expectation!

*(But it came to pass, that when Sanballat heard that we builded the wall, he was wroth, and took great indignation, and mocked the Jews. **2** And he spake before his brethren and the army of Samaria, and said, What do these feeble Jews? will they fortify themselves? will they sacrifice? will they make an end in a day? will they revive the stones out of the heaps of the rubbish which are burned? **3** Now Tobiah the Ammonite was by him, and he said, Even that which they build, if a fox go up, he shall even break down their stone wall. **4** Hear, O our God; for we are despised: and turn their reproach upon their own head, and give them for a prey in the land of captivity: **5** And cover not their iniquity, and let not their sin be blotted out from before thee: for they have provoked thee to anger before the builders. **6** So built we the wall; and all the wall was joined together unto the half thereof: for the people had a mind to work.**7** But it came to pass, that when Sanballat, and Tobiah, and the Arabians, and the Ammonites, and the Ashdodites, heard that the walls of Jerusalem*

*were made up, and that the breaches began to be
stopped, then they were very wroth, **8** And conspired
all of them together to come and to fight against
Jerusalem, and to hinder it. **9** Nevertheless we made
our prayer unto our God, and set a watch against
them day and night, because of them.) Neh 4:1-9
(KJV)*

Sanballat heard the wall was built and he was wroth, and took great indignation, and mocked the Jews. There will always be an opposing spirit trying to stop you from working for God. The enemy is mad because you made a decision to repair your life. He will oppose you and tell you "don't even start," "don't waste your time." If he can't stop you from starting, he will be back. The enemy will not leave you alone when you begin to work on your situation. He will hear about what you're doing. Someone is going to tell him you're doing alright, that you're growing in the things of the Lord and that you're looking better. News will get back to the enemy that you're no longer broken. He will come back to stop your progress. He will now try to hinder you with ridicule. Tobiah heard Sanballat's words of criticism and joined him. They began to belittle and criticize the great work that had been accomplished. Is the enemy so wroth with what you've accomplished that you would consider stopping? Can he convince you that you haven't made any progress and that nothing has really changed?

Nehemiah started this task with prayer and continued with prayer. *Prayer shows us the work to be done. When we are working towards something we should pray. Prayer invokes us to work. Anytime there's work to be done, there should be prayer. No prayer causes us to neglect work. Many of us aren't working because we aren't praying.* Nehemiah didn't get distracted from the work because of the enemy's ridicule. He prayed and kept working. Don't get angry and start exchanging words with the enemy. Overcome ridicule. We give the enemy too much power when we stop working and sit down because of someone's mouth! You may be ridiculed and despised but let those oppositions give you an opportunity to be faithful unto God, let it give you a mind to work. Despite the ridicule the wall was joined together unto the half. *(No weapon* [**the weapon of ridicule**] *that is formed against thee shall prosper; and every tongue that shall rise against thee in judgment thou shalt condemn.) Isaiah 54:17 (KJV)* [**How is it going to be condemned? By your works, your life, your prayers and right standing with God.**] **You don't have to defend yourself to the enemy.** You may have a mind to start something, but do you have a strong enough mind to complete what you started?

When you have a mind to work the work will get done. Don't be distracted by ridiculed. Stop being distracted by what's being said. Continue to hear God's voice over the voice of the enemy. When you have a mind to work for God the enemy will not be able to stop you. There are many people that can't take being talked about. If you can't stand ridicule you will not complete assignments. When breaches are stopped the enemy is wroth. He can no longer come into your marriage. He can no longer get into your finances. No more afflicting your body. Of course the enemy is wroth, his ultimate goal is to kill, to steal, and to destroy. When you stop the breaches the enemy will go to his next move. *Chapter 4:7 . . . Sanballat, Tobiah, and the Arabians, and the Ammonites, and the Ashdodites, heard that the walls of Jerusalem were made up, and that the breaches began to be stopped, then they were very wroth. Ain't nobody bad but the devil! And conspired all of them together to come and to fight Jerusalem, and to hinder it. v8* When the enemy wants to stop you, he will find those that share a dislike for you. They will join the campaign to stop you. The more work you accomplish there will be an increase in very wroth enemies. Knowing of the enemies plans to make war against them, Nehemiah prays to God. He uses the word nevertheless meaning in spite of that. I would like to say it like this, *whatever devil!* A watch is set day and night because of the enemy's threat of war. When the oppositions of disparagement, laughter, ridicule, and threats don't work the enemy may try to become physical. *(But I beseech you, that I may not be bold when I am present with that confidence, wherewith I think to be bold against some, which think of us as if we walked according to the flesh. 3 For though we walk in the flesh, we do not war after the flesh: 4 (For the weapons of our warfare are not carnal, but mighty through God to the pulling down of strong holds;) 2 Cor 10:2-4 (KJV)* Repeated reports of a sneak attack by the enemy kept the vigil going. The plans of the enemy did not work. When we open our ears naturally and spiritually, watch, and pray, we put ourselves in a position of awareness and readiness. *(Beloved, think it not strange concerning the fiery trial which is to try you, as though some strange thing happened unto you:) 1 Peter 4:12 (KJV)* Nehemiah refused to be discouraged or intimidated by internal difficulties or external threats against him.

Nehemiah positioned his workers after their families with their swords, their spears, and their bows. Sanballat and the others heard of the preparation. There was a no-show from the enemy and the workers went back to work. Don't take the enemy's threat lightly. When someone threatens you don't be a coward. Don't go somewhere and hide. Prepare yourself to fight for your life. Fight for your future. Fight for what God has said to you. No physical battle was fought. Why? When your heart is prepared to fight for the things of God, God is prepared to fight for you. He fought this battle by bringing the enemy's counsel to nought. *(When a man's ways please the* LORD, *he maketh even his enemies to be at peace with him.) Prov 16:7 (KJV)* Knowing that the work was great and large they continued the work. *And it came to pass from that time forth, that the half of the servants wrought in the work, and the other half of them held both the spears, the shields, and the bows, and the habergeons; … They which builded on the wall, and they that bare burdens, with those that laded, everyone with one of his hands wrought in the work, and with the other hand held a weapon. For the builders, everyone had his sword girded by his side, and so builded. … Neh 4:16-18 (KJV).* Watching and not putting their clothes off unless they put them off for washing and bathing themselves. We have to put our hand to the gospel plough and with the other hand hold our weapon. *(. . . , and the sword of the Spirit, which is the word of God:)Eph 6:17 (KJV)* WATCH AND PRAY! *(Watch and pray, that ye enter not into temptation: the spirit indeed is willing, but the flesh is weak.) Matt 26:41 (KJV)*

REFLECTION QUESTIONS

1. Has there ever been a time in your life you stopped an assignment or striving to get closer to God because of ridicule? Did the ridicule come from your friends or your enemies?
2. Have you given information about an assignment to the wrong person, only to see signs of sabotage from that individual or from others because they shared the information?
3. How do you prepare yourself when threatened and attacked verbally by the enemy?
4. Nehemiah prioritized the building of the gates. Have you tried to repair areas in your life from without with disregard to repairing the gate of your spiritual treasure within?
5. With all honesty how well do you work with others in helping them carry out their assignment for God?

PRAYER

Father, in the midst of the opposition of ridicule help me to stay focused on You. Nullify the voice of the enemy and cause Your voice to become loud in me. Help me to remain faithful to You. Help me to discern those that are for me and discern those that are against me. Open my ears to hear and my eyes to see. Shield me from the darts of the wicked. Allow the opposition of ridicule to draw me closer to You. Amen.

Conform (do the accepted thing) to the *opposition* or take the *opportunity* to transform (change)

2 And be not conformed to this world: but be ye transformed by the renewing of your mind, that ye may prove what *is* that good, and acceptable, and perfect, will of God. Romans 12:2 (KJV)

CHAPTER 3

Opt Out? Not an Option

So built we the wall; and all the wall was joined together unto the half thereof: for the people had a mind to work. Neh 4:6 (KJV)

8 And conspired all of them together to come and to fight against Jerusalem, and to hinder it. 9 Nevertheless we made our prayer unto our God, and set a watch against them day and night, because of them. 10 And Judah said, The strength of the bearers of burdens is decayed, and there is much rubbish; so that we are not able to build the wall. 11 And our adversaries said, They shall not know, neither see, till we come in the midst among them, and slay them, and cause the work to cease. 12 And it came to pass, that when the Jews which dwelt by them came, they said unto us ten times, From all places whence ye shall return unto us they will be upon you. 13 Therefore set I in the lower places behind the wall, and on the higher places, I even set the people after *their families with their swords, their spears, and their bows. **14** And I looked, and rose up, and said unto the nobles, and to the rulers, and to the rest of the people, Be not ye afraid of them: remember the Lord, which is great and terrible, and fight for your brethren, your sons, and your daughters, your wives, and your houses. **15** And it came to pass, when our enemies heard that it was known unto us, and God had brought their counsel to nought, that we returned all of us to the wall, every one unto his work. Neh 4:8-15 (KJV)*

16 *And it came to pass from that time forth, that the half of my servants wrought in the work, and the other half of them held both the spears, the shields, and the bows, and the habergeons; and the rulers were behind all the house of Judah. **17** They which builded on the wall, and they that bare burdens, with those that laded, every one with one of his hands wrought in the work, and with the other hand held a weapon. **18** For the builders, every one had his sword girded by his side, and so builded. And he that sounded the trumpet was by me. **19** And I said unto the nobles, and to the rulers, and to the rest of the people, The work is great and large, and we are separated upon the wall, one far from another. **20** In what place therefore ye hear the sound of the trumpet, resort ye thither unto us: our God shall fight for us. **21** So we laboured in the work: and half of them held the spears from the rising of the morning till the stars appeared. **22** Likewise at the same time said I unto the people, Let every one with* *his servant lodge within Jerusalem, that in the night they may be a guard to us, and labour on the day. 23 So neither I, nor my brethren, nor my servants, nor the men of the guard which followed me, none of us put off our clothes, saving that every one put them off for washing. Neh 4:16-23 (KJV)*

Anytime you want to do a work for God someone is going to oppose you. If they can't stop you by ridiculing you and opposing you they will start ridiculing what you're doing. They will say things like, "it isn't working," "it isn't happening," "I don't see any fruit from it." But you'd better let the devil know he is a lie, waiting to happen. You tell the enemy you may not see what God is doing right now, but you know God is working on it. You may not see the fruit of your labor but God promised you whatever you do in the name of Jesus it would be perpetual. *(Ye have not chosen me, but I have chosen you, and ordained you, that ye should go and bring forth fruit, and that your fruit should remain: that whatsoever ye shall ask of the Father in my name, he may give it you. 17 These things I command you, that ye love one another.) John 15:16-17 (KJV)* If you listen to what people say, if you go on what you see, you probably would have given up a long time ago. *(Therefore, my beloved brethren, be ye stedfast, unmoveable, always abounding in the work of the Lord, forasmuch as ye know that your labour is not in vain in the Lord.) 1 Cor 15:58 (KJV)* Thank God, that you will not be stopped because of opposition. The greatest thing you need to understand is that you can't stop working because someone opposes you. You can't stop working because someone doesn't like what you're doing. You can't stop working because someone is giving you a hard time. If anything, this opposition should provoke you to be more determined to work harder. Nehemiah said when the people had a mind to work . . . . It doesn't matter what the enemy does when you've got a mind to work. Some of us don't have a mind to work. When you really have a mind to do what God says or anything you want to do, whether you're out there in the world or in the church, it doesn't matter what anyone says, no one can talk you out of it.

Get to a place in God that when the enemy comes against you you're going to gird yourself. *(Put on the whole armour of God, that ye may be able to stand against the wiles of the devil.* **12** *For we wrestle not against flesh and blood, but against principalities, against powers, against the rulers of the darkness of this world, against spiritual wickedness in high places.* **13** *Wherefore take unto you the whole armour of God, that ye may be able to withstand in the evil day, and having done all, to stand.* **14** *Stand therefore, having your loins girt about with truth, and having on the breastplate of righteousness;* **15** *And your feet shod with the preparation of the gospel of peace;* **16** *Above all, taking the shield of faith, wherewith ye shall be able to quench all the fiery darts of the wicked.) Eph 6:11-16 (KJV)* We easily let the enemy talk us out of doing the will of God. Don't you let some doubting Thomas or some demon of influence that doesn't have your best spiritual will in mind talk you out of fulfilling your assignment. Many of us are around people of this sort at this very moment. They will end up talking you out of your assignment because your mind is not strong enough. *(I beseech you therefore, brethren, by the mercies of God, that ye present your bodies a living sacrifice, holy, acceptable unto God, which is your reasonable service.* **2** *And be not conformed to this world: but be ye transformed by the renewing of your mind, that ye may prove what is that good, and acceptable, and perfect, will of God.) Romans 12:1-2 (KJV)* You've got to renew your mind if you're going to work for God. It doesn't matter what the enemy says, it doesn't matter what the enemy does, no one can stop you from doing what God says if you really want to do it. Do you have a mind to work? Do you have a mind to advance? Do you have the mind to get where God wants you to be? It is so sad that we know where God wants us, we know what God has for us, but our mind isn't strong enough to make the journey. *(And take the helmet of salvation, and the sword of the Spirit, which is the word of God:) Eph 6:17 (KJV)* We have to have a mind to complete what we start. Don't stop doing what God wants you to do because of someone's foolishness, because of someone's stupidity, because of someone's ignorance. Don't allow these oppositions to get you out of the flow of the anointing of God and stop your hands from working. Carry out the assignment. Finish what you start.

When the enemy came and started threatening Nehemiah he got at the lower places behind the wall gate and put some people at the higher places behind the wall. They worked having their sword girded by their side. We should liken ourselves to this type of commitment. We cannot build our lives or the lives of others without having our sword. *(And take the helmet of salvation, and the sword of the Spirit, which is the word of God:) Eph 6:17 (KJV)* We've got to work for God and keep the sword at hand. When the enemy comes all we have to do is open our mouth and keep working. God is able to do what He says He's going to do. He is able to give you the strength. He is able to cause you to go through and prevail against the spirit of sabotage that accompanies the Sanballats, Tobiahs and Geshems in your life.

When you've done all you know to do. When something is blocking your path it gives you an opportunity to overcome. Overcoming is talking to and talking about God. Trusting Him to make a way. Opposition gives you an opportunity to allow God to show you what to do. If anybody's going to quit, let the devil quit.

REFLECTION QUESTIONS

1. Do you think God gives us an option to opt out?
2. If you felt some assignments were optional, would you say that the assignment was a good idea or a God idea?
3. When you realized that a spirit of sabotage was in operation during an assignment how did you handle it?

PRAYER

Father, regulate my mind. Speak to my heart. Help me to stay in the flow or your anointing and purpose. Increase my faith and remove all doubt. Help me to overcome the challenges that are trying to hinder my assignment. Allow the opposition of confrontation to strengthen my hands. Amen

CHAPTER 4

God Is More Real Than Fear (false evidence appearing real)

Think upon me, my God, for good, according to all that I have done for this people. Neh 5:19 (KJV)

Now it came to pass, when Sanballat, and Tobiah, and Geshem the Arabian, and the rest of our enemies, heard that I had builded the wall, and that there was no breach left therein; (though at that time I had not set up the doors upon the gates;) 2 That Sanballat and Geshem sent unto me, saying, Come, let us meet together in some one of the villages in the plain of Ono. But they thought to do me mischief. 3 And I sent messengers unto them, saying, I am doing a great work, so that I cannot come down: why should the work cease, whilst I leave it, and come down to you? 4 Yet they sent unto me four times after this sort; and I answered them after the same manner. 5 Then sent Sanballat his servant unto me in like manner the fifth time with an open letter in his hand; 6 Wherein was written, It is reported among the heathen, and Gashmu saith it, that thou and the Jews think to rebel: for which cause thou buildest the wall, that thou mayest be their king, according to these words. 7 And thou hast also appointed prophets to preach of thee at Jerusalem, saying, There is a king in Judah: and now shall it be reported to the king according to these words. Come now therefore, and let us take counsel together. 8 Then I sent unto him, saying, There are no such things done as thou sayest, but thou feignest them out of thine own heart. 9 For they all made us afraid, saying, Their hands shall be weakened from the work, that it be not done. Now therefore, O God, strengthen my hands. Neh 6:1-9 (KJV)

During opposition from the enemy some of the Jews were oppressed by their brethren. Nehemiah heard of the oppression. He put a stop to it. Nehemiah was faithful unto the building of the wall. He required nothing of the people because he didn't want to add to their oppression. His request for the work was that *Nehemiah 5:19 God think upon him, for good, according to all that he had done for this people.* We have enough problems with the enemy; surely we don't need to cause oppression with each other. The enemy will not stop trying to hinder the work of God. Sanballat, Tobiah, Geshem, and the rest of the enemies heard that the wall had been built with the exception of the doors upon the gates begin hung. You'd better know that your enemy keeps tabs on you. We can have the walls of our heart built up but we have to make sure that the gates are hung to our heart. Guard the entrance to your heart, through your ear and your eye gate. The gate is one of the most needed things for protection. Ask God to anoint your ears and our eyes. Turn a deaf ear to what the enemy is saying and continue to listen to God's instructions. See things the way God sees them. Keep your heart turn towards God and know that you're doing a great work.

So many of us stop what we're doing just to meet with the enemy. We already know the enemy has a problem with us. We already know the enemy has something against us. The enemy picks the meeting place. They wanted to meet Nehemiah and stop the work by assassinating him. The enemy wants to set you up. So he can kill your desires, your visions, your dreams, your hopes, your accomplishments, and put an end to your great work. Nehemiah was wise enough to say no. *("I am doing a great work, so that I cannot come down." Neh. 6:3)* You've got to think for yourself that you're doing something great. If no one thinks the work you're doing is worth something, you've got to feel that what you're doing is worth something. You have the voice of authority and you can tell the enemy NO. The enemy has enough sense to know that what you're doing is great enough to stop some of his work. *("Why should the work cease, whilst I leave it, and come down to you?" Neh. 6:3)* You have to have enough drive and enough passion in you that what you're doing has to continue until God tells you to stop. Until IT IS FINISHED! Christ's passion took Him to the cross and He hung there until IT WAS FINISHED! When we stop it's because we've given in to the oppositions. God is able to do what He said He would do. He's able to give you the strength you need. He's able to cause you to go through and prevail in everything that you put your hands to. We have so much unfinished work that we've started. *(They strengthened their hands. Neh. 6:9)* It is up to you to strengthen your hands. You've got to make up your mind that you're going to do what God says do and pray your way through. You have got to get determination in you and say, what I've started I have to finish.

Four times the message was sent to Nehemiah. The fifth time an open letter was sent. The enemy came four times and he's going to keep coming. He wears us down with his constant nagging and harassing until we give in. What are you going to say each time he comes? A letter of accusation is presented to Nehemiah. If the enemy can't get you to come down and do what he wants he will come with an accusation. This is another avenue he will use to get you distracted from your work. Come down, let the work cease while you defend yourself. You have to have self-control or you will find yourself following the words of people trying to convince them of your innocence. You've got to have discipline when people start running their mouths about you. If you don't have discipline you will be ready to take matters into your own hands. You will come down from your work. You will try to overcome accusations by getting on the phone. You may feel like becoming physical. You will want to say some things. You don't fight oppositions in this manner. *(For though we walk in the flesh, we do not war after the flesh:* **4** *(For the weapons of our warfare are not carnal, but mighty through God to the pulling down of strong holds;) 2 Cor 10:3-4 (KJV)* Why should the work cease? While the accusations and rumors are spreading, find yourself working. When something is said overcome it by praying.

Prayer will sustain you. When you have a prayer life you will not involve yourself in the situation. Remember when Jesus was in the Garden of Gethsemane, he told the disciples to watch and pray. He'd come back and they would be asleep. He told them to sleep on because they were neither watching nor praying. When you have a prayer life you have control. When the multitude came to take Jesus, the disciples jumped up and started fighting.

Peter cut off the high priest's servant's ear. *(Watch and pray, that ye enter not into temptation: the spirit indeed is willing, but the flesh is weak.) Matt 26:41 (KJV)* Your spirit wills to do things that your flesh will be in opposition to. The only thing that's going to subdue your flesh is prayer and the Word of God. The flesh will get you in trouble. It will keep you from working for God. That's why the Scripture says: *(This I say then, Walk in the Spirit, and ye shall not fulfil the lust of the flesh. 17 For the flesh lusteth against the Spirit, and the Spirit against the flesh: and these are contrary the one to the other: so that ye cannot do the things that ye would.) Gal 5:16-17 (KJV).* The accusations (opposition) allowed Nehemiah to have self-control but it also brought about fear *(false evidence appearing real).* Leaders and pastors have to have followers that are confident in the call of God on their life. How many lies, rumors, and accusations have caused faithful workers to leave ministry? How much *fear* has accusations brought to church members that they now renege on what they know to do? For they all made us afraid, saying, *(Their hands shall be weakened from the work, that it be not done. Now therefore, O God, strengthen my hands.) Neh 6:9 (KJV) Fear* will come with the accusations. Nehemiah had to pray for God's help in this situation. The accusations were serious. Has accusations of your leader made you afraid, and because of *fear* has your hands become weakened from the work, have you become discouraged and the work remains undone? Has the opposition of *fear* brought on by accusations weakened your hands, and you no longer work in your church? *Fear* will cause you to be discouraged. Discouragement causes work to cease. *(For God hath not given us the spirit of fear; but of power, and of love, and of a sound mind.) 2 Tim 1:7 (KJV)*

Afterward I came unto the house of Shemaiah the son of Delaiah the son of Mehetabeel, who was shut up; and he said, Let us meet together in the house of God, within the temple, and let us shut the doors of the temple: for they will come to slay thee; yea, in the night will they come to slay thee. 11 And I said, Should such a man as I flee? and who is there, that, being as I am, would go into the temple to save his life? I will not go in. 12 And, lo, I perceived that God had not sent him; but that he pronounced this prophecy against me: for Tobiah and Sanballat had hired him. 13 Therefore was he hired, that I should be afraid, and do so, and sin, and that they might have matter for an evil report, that they might reproach me. 14 My God, think thou upon Tobiah and Sanballat according to these their works, and on the prophetess Noadiah, and the rest of the prophets, that would have put me in fear. 15 So the wall was finished in the twenty and fifth day of the month Elul, in fifty and two days. 16 And it came to pass, that when all our enemies heard thereof, and all the heathen that were about us saw these things, they were much cast down in their own eyes: for they perceived that this work was wrought of our God. Neh 6:10-16 (KJV)

The enemy tries to set Nehemiah up. Shemaiah gives him a word that Nehemiah perceived was not from God. When you walk close to God, he will give you discernment. *(My sheep hear my voice, and I know them, and they follow me:) John 10:27 (KJV)* Hired by Tobiah and Sanballat that he should be afraid, and do so and sin. *Fear* will cause you to sin. Sin brings reproach. You've got to be above reproach when you're working for God. Leadership is a great position, it's a powerful position. You can build or tear down. You can cause life or death. Your life has to be an example of faith and confidence in God and not an example of *fear* and distrust. Nehemiah was strengthened in this and declared that he would not sin by fleeing into the house of God by believing a false report that could bring an evil report against him. Keep working and God will take care of the situation. Nehemiah does what he had always done, pray. He asked God to think on the ones that had tried to put *fear* in him. *Fear* comes to get you to stop working. Regardless of the tactic of *fear* from the enemy, in 52 days the work was finished. What you thought should have taken longer won't take as long because you have a mind to work. When the enemies of the Jews saw it *they were much cast down in their own eyes.* They couldn't believe what they saw. It blew their mind. They perceived that this work was wrought of God. People have got to see the manifestation of God in your life. Take the opposition of *fear* and give the enemies eyes a chance to see the finished work that God is working through you.

REFLECTION QUESTIONS

1. How do you feel when accusations and rumors are spread about you?
2. Are there any uncompleted assignments present in your life because of distraction(s)?
3. Has your life been an example of faith and confidence in God, or an example of fear and distrust?

PRAYER

Father, help me to follow your instructions. Anoint my ears and my eyes to recognize and avoid distractions. Place a passion in me for the things of God. Allow the opposition of fear and accusations to strengthen my confidence in You. Amen

The closer He (Jesus) gets the better you'll look. Opposition has a way of changing our state of being to becoming or shaping us to the very thing that opposes us. Bitterness, hatred, anger, resentment, etc. Take the opposition and do the opposite.

CHAPTER 5

Challenges

There was a man in the land of Uz, whose name was Job; and that man was perfect and upright, and one that feared God, and eschewed evil. Job 1:1 (KJV)

God's Testimony of Job: ***Now there was a day*** *when the sons of God came to present themselves before the LORD, and Satan came also among them. 7 And the LORD said unto Satan, Whence comest thou? Then Satan answered the LORD, and said, From going to and fro in the earth, and from walking up and down in it.* **8 And the LORD said unto Satan, Hast thou considered my servant Job, that there is none like him in the earth, a perfect and an upright man, one that feareth God, and escheweth evil?** *9 Then Satan answered the LORD, and said, Doth Job fear God for nought? 10 Hast not thou made an hedge about him, and about his house, and about all that he hath on every side? thou hast blessed the work of his hands, and*

*his substance is increased in the land. **11** But put
forth thine hand now, and touch all that he hath,
and he will curse thee to thy face. **12** And the LORD
said unto Satan, Behold, all that he hath is in thy
power; only upon himself put not forth thine hand.
So Satan went forth from the presence of the LORD.
Job 1:6-12 (KJV)*

Satan appearing before God, questioning Job's sincerity
towards God; obtains permission to oppose Job. Job was no
ordinary man. He was a highly favored individual. He had wealth,
prosperity, many possessions, a fine family, and most of all Job
was a godly man. He feared the Lord. Job was tried through
the circumstances of his own life. Satan's objective in attacking
your circumstances is to destroy your relationship with God and
to *alienate you from God. Satan's objective: (1) to cause you
to question God's love. (2) to cause you to lose faith in God's
promises. Satan wants to gain your will so that you will turn
your back on God and turn against Him. Keep in mind you're
being backstabbed by Satan, he will turn you against God, when
he is the one bringing the oppositions. Satan is the one with the
diabolical schemes. *(And I heard a loud voice saying in heaven, Now
is come salvation, and strength, and the kingdom of our God, and
the power of his Christ: for the accuser of our brethren is cast down,
which accused them before our God day and night.) Rev 12:10 (KJV)*

---

*   challenge—a calling into question, a call or dare to take part in a
     duel, contest, etc.; anything, such as a demanding task that calls
     for special effort or dedication.

**   alienate—make unfriendly, set against, push away, separate from,
     turn away from, turn your back on.

Behind every circumstance, every trial, and every opposition there is a significant reason. Often we are not able to see that reason or comprehend it through our natural senses. During your circumstances you find your thoughts are not always clear. The following scripture was written for Israel during their Babylonian captivity but you can apply this scripture to your circumstances. *(For I know the thoughts that I think toward you, saith the* LORD, *thoughts of peace, and not of evil, to give you an expected end.) Jer 29:11 (KJV)* All you know is what's going on right now, what you want right now and what you're feeling right now. Again, I repeat, behind every circumstance, every trial, and every opposition there is a significant reason. Having a problem with NOW, NOW, NOW, is going to cause you a lot of unnecessary grief if you don't recognize what's going on. You've got a choice, you can keep your eyes on your circumstance and succumb to it or you can trust GOD with your life, while in your circumstance.

We do not live in one world at a time. We live simultaneously in two worlds; the physical-world and the spirit-world. The physical world is a materialistic, human, flesh and blood world. The spirit world (unseen world) is the realm of the spirits, angels, demons, the supernatural, etc . . . The spirit-world is just as real as the physical-world, understandably, more so. *While we look not at the things which are seen, but at the things which are not seen: for the things which are seen are temporal; but the things which are not seen are eternal. 2 Cor 4:18 (KJV)* Jobs trials and oppositions took place in both of these worlds, as do ours. He knew that the spiritual world of faith consists of more than what he saw or what he possessed.

Job is a classic example of the attacks of oppositions in the circumstances of life. The bible tells us that Job was an upright man, perfect in his ways. It was Satan's contention that God had blessed and guarded Job; as you would expect him to be perfect, upright, fear God and avoid evil. Satan challenged God to take away this hedge of protection, allow him to attack Job; surely Job would rebel against God and curse God. God rose to the challenge. With God's permission Satan was allowed to bring oppositions; through situations, conditions, state of affairs, status and position. With Job it was one loss after another. He lost his possessions, his servants, his children, and his house. Throughout this ordeal Job sinned not nor charged God foolishly. *(And there was a day when his sons and his daughters were eating and drinking wine in their eldest brother's house: 14 And there came a messenger unto Job, and said, The oxen were plowing, and the asses feeding beside them: 15 And the Sabeans fell upon them, and took them away; yea, they have slain the servants with the edge of the sword; and I only am escaped alone to tell thee. 16 While he was yet speaking, there came also another, and said, The fire of God is fallen from heaven, and hath burned up the sheep, and the servants, and consumed them; and I only am escaped alone to tell thee. 17 While he was yet speaking, there came also another, and said, The Chaldeans made out three bands, and fell upon the camels, and have carried them away, yea, and slain the servants with the edge of the sword; and I only am escaped alone to tell thee. 18 While he was yet speaking, there came also another, and said, Thy sons and thy daughters were eating and drinking wine in their eldest brother's house: 19 And, behold, there came a great wind from the wilderness, and smote the four corners of the house, and it fell upon the young men, and they are dead; and I only am escaped alone to tell thee. 20 Then Job arose, and rent his mantle, and shaved his head, and fell down upon the ground, and worshipped, 21 And said, Naked came I out of my mother's womb, and naked shall I return thither: the LORD gave, and the LORD hath taken away; blessed be the name of the LORD. 22 In all this Job sinned not, nor charged God foolishly.) Job 1:13-22 (KJV)* Along with the loss of his possessions, wealth and children, in his mourning Job took the opportunity to exalt God above his circumstances.

> God's Testimony of Job: *__Again there was a day__ when the sons of God came to present themselves before the L<small>ORD</small>, and Satan came also among them to present himself before the L<small>ORD</small>. 2 And the L<small>ORD</small> said unto Satan, From whence comest thou? And Satan answered the L<small>ORD</small>, and said, From going to and fro in the earth, and from walking up and down in it. 3* Satan is a supernatural being opposing the will of God.*4 And Satan answered the L<small>ORD</small>, and said, Skin for skin, yea, all that a man hath will he give for his life. 5 But put forth thine hand now, and touch his bone and his flesh, and he will curse thee to thy face. 6 And the L<small>ORD</small> said unto Satan, Behold, he is in thine hand; but save his life. 7 So went Satan forth from the presence of the L<small>ORD</small>, and smote Job with sore boils from the sole of his foot unto his crown. 8 And he took him a potsherd to scrape himself withal; and he sat down among the ashes. 9 Then said his wife unto him, Dost thou still retain thine integrity? curse God, and die. 10 But he said unto her, Thou speakest as one of the foolish women speaketh. What? shall we receive good at the hand of God, and shall we not receive evil? In all this did not Job sin with his lips. Job 2:1-10 (KJV)*

Satan, appearing again before God, obtains further permission to test Job. Notice God uses the word "still" in verse three. Saying to Satan concerning the first challenge; even now, in spite of everything, nevertheless, nonetheless, however, notwithstanding, yet Job holds firmly to his integrity; although you moved me against him, to destroy him without a reason. Satan is allowed to attack Job's health. The affliction of Job's body with boils caused him much suffering and pain. His life became so miserable with this affliction that he cursed the day he was born. He took a potsherd to scrape himself with. *(And he took him a potsherd to scrape himself withal; and he sat down among the ashes.) Job 2:8 (KJV)* He had restless nights, tossing to and fro, broken skin, running sores, *(When I lie down, I say, When shall I arise, and the night be gone? and I am full of tossings to and fro unto the dawning of the day. 5 My flesh is clothed with worms and clods of dust; my skin is broken, and become loathsome.) Job 7:4-5 (KJV)* Job was so filled with disease and corruption that it seemed he was being munched through like a moth-eaten garment. *(And he, as a rotten thing, consumeth, as a garment that is moth eaten.) Job 13:28 (KJV)* He was wrinkled and thin. *(And thou hast filled me with wrinkles, which is a witness against me: and my leanness rising up in me beareth witness to my face.) Job 16:8 (KJV)* His face was sallow. *(My face is foul with weeping, and on my eyelids is the shadow of death;) Job 16:16 (KJV)* He was very thin; you could see the shape of his bones. *(My bone cleaveth to my skin and to my flesh, and I am escaped with the skin of my teeth.) Job 19:20 (KJV)* He had chronic gnawing pain. *(My bones are pierced in me in the night season: and my sinews take no rest.) Job 30:17 (KJV)* His skin color was altered. He was feverish. *(My skin is black upon me, and my bones are burned with heat.) Job 30:30 (KJV)*

In these challenges between God and Satan, Job's faith in God and love for God was being tested. God allowed the oppositions to prove Job's faith and love for Him. Satan used the oppositions to disprove God's testimony of Job; God tested his faith to prove it. God allowed Satan to proceed with limitations to accomplish the test but not to destroy Job. God allowed the test which proved Job's faithfulness and validity. Always remember Satan can do no more to you than God allows. When going through trials it is somewhat like a traffic signal. The green light permits Satan to go forth with his plans. The yellow light has established limitations as to what he is allowed to do. The red light demands him to stop his attacks.

Satan is a supernatural being opposing the will of God. He tempts you to destroy your faith. Trials are a must. When met with joy, trials produce endurance which in turn produces maturity. Just as Simon couldn't purchase the Holy Spirit with money, you cannot purchase maturity. Oppositions give you a chance to grow. Grow up: naturally and spiritually.

REFLECTION QUESTIONS

1. Have any of the trials that you've been through caused you to question God's love, or caused you to lose faith in God's promises?
2. Have you ever felt like you've been through hell and back, the devil couldn't kill you, but you were surprised what you could live through? Circumstances of life that you never thought or expected would happen to you.
3. During a trial, did you discern the significant reason while in the trial or at the end of the trial?
4. In reference to question #3, do you believe your outcome would have been different had you known the purpose of the trial?
5. Have you matured because of some of the oppositions you have faced in the circumstances of your life?

PRAYER

Father, Help me to be strong in my faith when I am faced with challenges in life. Whenever my faith is tested, whenever my love is on trial, whatever oppositions that afflict me in life help me to be sincere in my relationship with You. In my trials help me to grow naturally and spiritually. Amen.

CHAPTER 6

No Limit

You are not excluded from trials because you are born-again. Job is a perfect example of that. Satan didn't ask to try Job, God knew Satan had well thought-out Job's life and reasoned that was the reason Job reverenced God so. God allowed the challenges because of Satan's accusations. Certainly you won't face the trials Job went through, but when Satan has well thought-out your life; would you be up for the challenge? What would God's testimony be of you? Isn't it good to know that when your life pleases God, before, during, and after oppositions, God will withhold no good thing from them that walk upright *(For the LORD God is a sun and shield: the LORD will give grace and glory: no good thing will he withhold from them that walk uprightly.* **12** *O LORD of hosts, blessed is the man that trusteth in thee.) Psalms 84:11-12 (KJV)*

There were many statements of condemnation made towards Job. Eventually Job got his eyes on his circumstances. Being human, in a prolonged adverse situation he began to become weak and discouraged. So discouraged he cursed the day he was given life. *(After this opened Job his mouth, and cursed his day.* **2** *And Job* *spake, and said, 3 Let the day perish wherein I was born, and the night in which it was said, There is a man child conceived. 4 Let that day be darkness; let not God regard it from above, neither let the light shine upon it. 5 Let darkness and the shadow of death stain it; let a cloud dwell upon it; let the blackness of the day terrify it. 6 As for that night, let darkness seize upon it; let it not be joined unto the days of the year, let it not come into the number of the months. 7 Lo, let that night be solitary, let no joyful voice come therein. 8 Let them curse it that curse the day, who are ready to raise up their mourning. 9 Let the stars of the twilight thereof be dark; let it look for light, but have none; neither let it see the dawning of the day: 10 Because it shut not up the doors of my mother's womb, nor hid sorrow from mine eyes. 11 Why died I not from the womb? why did I not give up the ghost when I came out of the belly?) Job 3:1-11 (KJV)* He is confused and doubtful of answered prayer. *(If I had called, and he had answered me; yet would I not believe that he had hearkened unto my voice.) Job 9:16 (KJV)* Job became bitter as we sometimes do in our trials. In his bitterness he accuses God of injustice, oppression, and being unmerciful. Though he accused God of some things, he still maintains faith in spite of accusations of God as the cause of his sufferings. *(For I know that my redeemer liveth, and that he shall stand at the latter day upon the earth: 26 And though after my skin worms destroy this body, yet in my flesh shall I see God: 27 Whom I shall see for myself, and mine eyes shall behold, and not another; though my reins be consumed within me.) Job 19:25-27 (KJV)* Job remained in this state of mind until God dealt with him concerning his accusations towards Him. *(Moreover the* LORD *answered Job, and said, 2 Shall he that contendeth with the Almighty instruct him? he that reproveth God, let him answer it. 3 Then Job answered the* LORD, *and said, 4 Behold, I am vile; what shall I answer thee? I will lay mine hand upon my mouth. 5 Once have I spoken; but I will not answer: yea, twice; but I will proceed no further.) Job 40:1-5 (KJV)* Job humbles himself to God. He is now submitted to God.

> *Then Job answered the LORD, and said, 2 I know that thou canst do every thing, and that no thought can be withholden from thee. 3 Who is he that hideth counsel without knowledge? therefore have I uttered that I understood not; things too wonderful for me, which I knew not. 4 Hear, I beseech thee, and I will speak: I will demand of thee, and declare thou unto me. 5 I have heard of thee by the hearing of the ear: but now mine eye seeth thee. 6 Wherefore I abhor myself, and repent in dust and ashes. Job 42:1-6 (KJV)*

> *And the LORD turned the captivity of Job, when he prayed for his friends: also the LORD gave Job twice as much as he had before. 11 Then came there unto him all his brethren, and all his sisters, and all they that had been of his acquaintance before, and did eat bread with him in his house: and they bemoaned him, and comforted him over all the evil that the LORD had brought upon him: every man also gave him a piece of money, and every one an earring of gold. 12 So the LORD blessed the latter end of Job more than his beginning: for he had fourteen thousand sheep, and six thousand camels, and a thousand yoke of oxen, and a thousand she asses. 13 He had also seven sons and three daughters. 14 And he called the name of the first, Jemima; and*

the name of the second, Kezia; and the name of the third, Kerenhappuch. 15 And in all the land were no women found so fair as the daughters of Job: and their father gave them inheritance among their brethren. 16 After this lived Job an hundred and forty years, and saw his sons, and his sons' sons, even four generations. 17 So Job died, being old and full of days. Job 42:10-17 (KJV)

Job repented! God was free to move on his behalf. Repentance was the key to releasing God's blessings once more upon his life. God restored double what Satan had destroyed. God used all the circumstances Satan had used to defeat Job; healed him and blessed him materially beyond anything he had experienced before his trial. God magnifies and blesses Job. There was justice for Job after the accusations from Satan!

The bible says double. You may lose your job, your home, your husband, your wife, etc . . . , don't think it is the end of the world. You serve a God that has no limit. Count it all joy! Joy doesn't come because of the situation you're in or because of the circumstance. It doesn't come because of the pain and suffering. Neither does it come because of the opposition. If you lack wisdom in what you're going through, ask God. Don't be indecisive about asking. Be ready to accept His answer when he tells you. Joy comes because you have made an intelligent assessment of the truth of God's Word in your circumstance. (*My brethren, count it all joy when ye fall into divers temptations; 3 Knowing this, that the trying of your faith worketh patience. 4 But let patience have her perfect work, that ye may be perfect and entire, wanting nothing. 5 If any of you lack wisdom, let him ask of God, that giveth to all men liberally, and upbraideth not; and it shall be given him. 6 But let him ask in faith, nothing wavering. For he that wavereth is like a wave of the sea driven with the wind and tossed. 7 For let not that man think that he shall receive any thing of the Lord.) James 1:2-7 (KJV)*

In your trials, you may have been down for the count, but you weren't counted out. Family and friends may have given up on you; you may have given up on yourself. Your prolonged situation may have made you feel like you can't make it through; the outcome appears bleak. A trial is from day to day, you don't know when it will end. It may last for weeks, for months, or for years, but it will end. Your circumstance is God's opportunity to deliver you. *(Many are the afflictions of the righteous: but the LORD delivereth him out of them all.) Psalms 34:19 (KJV)*

REFLECTION QUESTIONS

1. Have any of your trials led you to question your existence?
2. Have you ever found yourself complaining and accusing God, but trying to maintain your faith?
3. Have you been through a trial that has caused you become bitter towards God?
4. Have you ever accused God of causing you to suffer only to learn later it was not of God but of Satan?
5. Have you been through a trial and God restored everything that was lost? Did He give you double for your trouble?

PRAYER

Father, I thank You for my birth. Thank You for every test and trial that I've gone through. Thank You for taking away the bitterness, and making me better. Thank You for the experience of knowing You as a deliverer and a restorer. Amen.

CHAPTER 7

The Dream is Not Theirs to Kill

(And Joseph dreamed a dream, and he told it his brethren: and they hated him yet the more. **6** *And he said unto them, Hear, I pray you, this dream which I have dreamed:* **7** *For, behold, we were binding sheaves in the field, and, lo, my sheaf arose, and also stood upright; and, behold, your sheaves stood round about, and made obeisance to my sheaf.* **8** *And his brethren said to him, Shalt thou indeed reign over us? or shalt thou indeed have dominion over us? And they hated him yet the more for his dreams, and for his words.* **9** *And he dreamed yet another dream, and told it his brethren, and said, Behold, I have dreamed a dream more; and, behold, the sun and the moon and the eleven stars made obeisance to me.* **10** *And he told it to his father, and to his brethren: and his father rebuked him, and said unto him, What is this dream that thou hast dreamed? Shall I and thy mother and thy brethren indeed come to bow down ourselves to thee to the earth?* **11** *And*

*his brethren envied him; but his father observed the
saying.) Gen 37:5-11 (KJV)*

The life of Joseph powerfully displays God's sovereign ability
to bring to pass His destiny for an obedient individual. In his
youth, Joseph received a vision of God's plan for his life. Shortly
thereafter it appeared that not only had the vision died, but that
the life of Joseph would be wasted away in slavery and prison.
Nevertheless, Joseph remained faithful to God. What had been
meant for evil, God used to prepare and position His servant to
realize the fulfillment of the vision for his life. *(And Joseph said
unto them, Fear not: for am I in the place of God? 20 But as for you,
ye thought evil against me; but God meant it unto good, to bring to
pass, as it is this day, to save much people alive.) Gen 50:19-20 (KJV).*
[The Genesis 50/20 Principle] If the devil had known, he would
have left you alone!

There may and will be times in your life as you mature in your
relationship with God you will learn what to share and when to
share with others. This was a significant dream from God. As
a youth, Joseph knew God had something special in mind for
him. Knowing this, he shared his dream prematurely. Ponder
God's vision. Do not share it prematurely, but ask God for His
timing. Although Joseph dreamed of his promotion, he had not
sensed that he was headed into a series of serious demotions on
the journey up. He did not anticipate the oppositions he would
come to encounter. It is already acknowledged in scriptures that
Joseph, characterized as a model boy was already in the habit of
telling his father the evil doings of his brothers as youths. Being
a tattle-tale put a strain on his relationship with his brothers. He
was also hated by his brothers because his father loved him more
than all his children: Joseph was the son of his old age. *(These*

are the generations of Jacob. Joseph, being seventeen years old, was feeding the flock with his brethren; and the lad was with the sons of Bilhah, and with the sons of Zilpah, his father's wives: and Joseph brought unto his father their evil report. 3 Now Israel loved Joseph more than all his children, because he was the son of his old age: and he made him a coat of many colours. 4 And when his brethren saw that their father loved him more than all his brethren, they hated him, and could not speak peaceably unto him.) Gen 37:2-4 (KJV)
Understandably, Benjamin was born about 9 years after Joseph. Joseph was the son especially devoted to the care of Jacob in his old age. With the death of Rachel, Joseph probably grew closer by assisting his father in supplying his wants and no doubt was a messenger between Jacob and his other sons. Attributing to the hatred was the fact that Jacob was unwise in showing a respect of persons as well as lessening his sons respect for him. Children are not blind to how other siblings are treated. Showing respect of persons amongst your children can and will cause envy, jealousy, rivalry (opposition), and trouble in the family. Though children may be sheltered, protected, and favored by their parents, when there is a call on their life and their destiny awaits them appointed by God, parents will not be able to control the oppositions that will confront them on their way to what God has planned for their life. Jacob rightly observed his son's dream as referring to himself and his family. The interpretation of the dream that they would be dependent upon Joseph and humbled before him.

The assignment to Shechem brought Joseph providentially to Dotham, a spot more convenient for contact with merchants using the main trade route on their way to Egypt. No doubt Joseph was gifted with dreams and divine interpretation. One thing you must learn concerning spiritual gifts, God grants them to whom He pleases. Joseph's brothers displayed oppositions of hatred, malice, envy, jealousy, mockery, ridicule, etc. which led to the conspiracy to take his life. Unfortunately we find this type of behavior in our birth/church families. The time to deal with envy and jealousy is when it first rears its' ugly head. The very one you resent and try to rid the family of may be your Joseph in your time of famine. That person as God did with Joseph to preserve the life of Israel may be the agent to preserve your life. *(And Joseph said unto his brethren, Come near to me, I pray you. And they came near. And he said, I am Joseph your brother, whom ye sold into Egypt. 5 Now therefore be not grieved, nor angry with yourselves, that ye sold me hither: for God did send me before you to preserve life.) Gen 45:4-5 (KJV)*

Genesis chapter 37 concludes with the facts that Joseph brothers kidnapped him with the intention to kill him. Sarcastically with contempt, look who is here, "this dreamer." *(And when they saw him afar off, even before he came near unto them, they conspired against him to slay him. 19 And they said one to another, Behold, this dreamer cometh. 20 Come now therefore, and let us slay him, and cast him into some pit, and we will say, Some evil beast hath devoured him: and we shall see what will become of his dreams.) Gen 37:18-20 (KJV)* Joseph is stripped of his coat of many colors, cast into a pit, lifted out the pit, sold into slavery into Egypt by his brothers. No matter what plans man may have for you, he may invent a situation but you serve a God that knows how to invade that situation. Man may have a plan for you and put it into action, but you serve a God that knows how to counteract that plan. Although Joseph's brothers did not kill him outright, they placed his life in someone else's hand. They were quite willing to let someone else do their dirty work. They thought they would never see "this dreamer" again. But God was in control of Joseph's life and had other plans. Joseph was soon to learn a key life lesson:

you may not see the road you will travel to reach your destiny; but God's promise will be fulfilled. When it looks like things are going contrary to your dream/vision that God has shown you, close your eyes and say with sincerity in your heart; God promised me. Survive the indifference while in the pit. Don't allow someone to kill what they didn't birth in you. The dream is not theirs to kill.

REFLECTION QUESTIONS

1. Did you receive a vision from God for your life? Are you fulfilling that vision at this present time?
2. We've all had dreams that bewilder us. Can you distinguish the difference between divine dreams from God or do you have dreams seeking interpretation from others?
3. Have you allowed someone to kill your dream?
4. Did you notice something different about yourself growing up as a child?

PRAYER

Father, as I grow in You, help me to be wise in my conversations. Help me to be certain of the plans You have for me. No matter how dark the pit, strengthen me, bring light to the dream. Amen.

CHAPTER 8

Other Plans

(And Joseph was brought down to Egypt; and Potiphar, an officer of Pharaoh, captain of the guard, an Egyptian, bought him of the hands of the Ishmeelites, which had brought him down thither. 2 And the LORD *was with Joseph, and he was a prosperous man; and he was in the house of his master the Egyptian. 3 And his master saw that the* LORD *was with him, and that the* LORD *made all that he did to prosper in his hand. 4 And Joseph found grace in his sight, and he served him: and he made him overseer over his house, and all that he had he put into his hand. 5 And it came to pass from the time that he had made him overseer in his house, and over all that he had, that the* LORD *blessed the Egyptian's house for Joseph's sake; and the blessing of the* LORD *was upon all that he had in the house, and in the field. 6 And he left all that he had in Joseph's hand; and he knew not ought he had, save the bread*

*which he did eat. And Joseph was a goodly person,
and well favoured.) Gen 39:1-6 (KJV)*

The key to Joseph's whole life is expressed in the words "the Lord was with him, and . . ." *(And the LORD was with Joseph, and he was a prosperous man; and he was in the house of his master the Egyptian. 3 And his master saw that the LORD was with him, and that the LORD made all that he did to prosper in his hand.) Gen 39:2-3 (KJV)* Any and all ideas that Joseph, twice the victim of injustice, had been abandoned by the Lord are eventually banished by statements of facts highlighting God's oversight of his opposing circumstances, "with him,"(v 3, 39:23), "with Joseph," 39:21), "made all he did prosper,"(v3), "made it to prosper,"(39:23), "found grace," (v4), "gave him favor," (39:21), "blessed/blessing of the Lord," (v5) and "showed him mercy,"(39:21). Neither being unjustly sold into slavery and forcibly removed from the Land (37:28), nor being unjustly accused of sexual harassment and imprisoned(39:7-20) were events signaling even a temporary loss of divine superintendence of Joseph's life and God's purpose for His people, Israel. Joseph had lived as a nomad, traveling the countryside with the family, caring for sheep. Suddenly he was thrust into the world's most advanced civilization with great pyramids, beautiful homes, sophisticated people, and a new language. While Joseph, a Hebrew saw Egypt's skill and intelligence at their best, he also saw the Egyptians spiritual blindness. They worshipped countless gods related to every aspect of life. Joseph lost no opportunity amid oppositions for speaking to them about God. He always spoke of the God of Israel, giving glory to Him and expressing absolute faith in His power and faithfulness. Being carried off into slavery was his training ground in learning a new culture. Expect God's favor in the sight of others, He is able to make a way when it seems impossible. Though opposition put him in prison, it positioned him to be placed in the position to fulfill the plan of God. Thirteen years have gone by, Joseph is made second ruler of all the land of Egypt. Joseph was experiencing the fulfillment of the Abrahamic Covenant, even at that time before Israel was in the land. *(And he said unto Abram, Know of a surety that thy seed shall be a stranger in a land that is not theirs, and shall serve them; and they shall afflict them four hundred years; 14 And also that nation, whom they shall serve, will I judge: and afterward shall they come out with great substance. 15 And thou shalt go to thy fathers in peace; thou shalt be buried in a good old age. 16 But in the fourth generation they shall come hither again: for the iniquity of the Amorites is not yet full.) Gen 15:13-16 (KJV)* Joseph was able to save a nation by translating God's plan for Egypt into practical actions. This was done by "this dreamer" that interpreted the Pharaoh's dream. It was a dream that got him into this situation and it was a dream that got him out of it. What a difference a day makes. Joseph rose to the top, from prison walls to Pharaoh's Palace.

His training along with his gift for this important position involved being first a slave and then a prisoner. In each situation he learned the importance of serving God and others. Whatever your situation, no matter how undesirable, consider it a part of your training program for fulfilling God's plan. God's plan is not dictated by human actions; they are only tools. By the time Joseph's troubles came to an end, God had given him the wisdom to understand that his rejection, slavery, and imprisonment had accomplished the purposes of God for his entire family.

> *Then Joseph could not refrain himself before all them*
> *that stood by him; and he cried, Cause every man to*
> *go out from me. And there stood no man with him,*

while Joseph made himself known unto his brethren.
2 And he wept aloud: and the Egyptians and the
house of Pharaoh heard. 3 And Joseph said unto his
brethren, I am Joseph; doth my father yet live? And
his brethren could not answer him; for they were
troubled at his presence. 4 And Joseph said unto his
brethren, Come near to me, I pray you. And they
came near. And he said, I am Joseph your brother,
whom ye sold into Egypt. 5 Now therefore be not
grieved, nor angry with yourselves, that ye sold me
hither: for God did send me before you to preserve
life. 6 For these two years hath the famine been in
the land: and yet there are five years, in the which
there shall neither be earing nor harvest. 7 And God
sent me before you to preserve you a posterity in the
earth, and to save your lives by a great deliverance.
8 So now it was not you that sent me hither, but
God: and he hath made me a father to Pharaoh, and
lord of all his house, and a ruler throughout all the
land of Egypt. 9 Haste ye, and go up to my father,
and say unto him, Thus saith thy son Joseph, God
hath made me lord of all Egypt: come down unto
me, tarry not: 10 And thou shalt dwell in the land
of Goshen, and thou shalt be near unto me, thou,
and thy children, and thy children's children, and
thy flocks, and thy herds, and all that thou hast:
11 And there will I nourish thee; for yet there are
five years of famine; lest thou, and thy household,
and all that thou hast, come to poverty. 12 And,
behold, your eyes see, and the eyes of my brother
Benjamin, that it is my mouth that speaketh unto

you. **13** *And ye shall tell my father of all my glory in Egypt, and of all that ye have seen; and ye shall haste and bring down my father hither.* **14** *And he fell upon his brother Benjamin's neck, and wept; and Benjamin wept upon his neck.* **15** *Moreover he kissed all his brethren, and wept upon them: and after that his brethren talked with him.* **16** *And the fame thereof was heard in Pharaoh's house, saying, Joseph's brethren are come: and it pleased Pharaoh well, and his servants.* **17** *And Pharaoh said unto Joseph, Say unto thy brethren, This do ye; lade your beasts, and go, get you unto the land of Canaan;* **18** *And take your father and your households, and come unto me: and I will give you the good of the land of Egypt, and ye shall eat the fat of the land.* **19** *Now thou art commanded, this do ye; take you wagons out of the land of Egypt for your little ones, and for your wives, and bring your father, and come.* **20** *Also regard not your stuff; for the good of all the land of Egypt is yours.* **21** *And the children of Israel did so: and Joseph gave them wagons, according to the commandment of Pharaoh, and gave them provision for the way.* **22** *To all of them he gave each man changes of raiment; but to Benjamin he gave three hundred pieces of silver, and five changes of raiment.* **23** *And to his father he sent after this manner; ten asses laden with the good things of Egypt, and ten she asses laden with corn and bread and meat for his father by the way.* **24** *So he sent his brethren away, and they departed: and he said unto them, See that ye fall not out by the way.* **25** *And they went up out* *of Egypt, and came into the land of Canaan unto Jacob their father, 26 And told him, saying, Joseph is yet alive, and he is governor over all the land of Egypt. And Jacob's heart fainted, for he believed them not. 27 And they told him all the words of Joseph, which he had said unto them: and when he saw the wagons which Joseph had sent to carry him, the spirit of Jacob their father revived: 28 And Israel said, It is enough; Joseph my son is yet alive: I will go and see him before I die. Gen 45:1-28 (KJV)*

Twenty two years later, "this dreamer" reveals his identity to his brothers. The dream is not dead. The dreamer is able to forgive his brothers for their cruel behavior towards him. Joseph is in a position to supply all the wants of Jacob's tribe. He sent word to his father knowing that his father would understand that his prophetic dream had been fulfilled (v 45:13) after his brothers told him what they saw. *(And he told it to his father, and to his brethren: and his father rebuked him, and said unto him, What is this dream that thou hast dreamed? Shall I and thy mother and thy brethren indeed come to bow down ourselves to thee to the earth? 11 And his brethren envied him; but his father observed the saying.) Gen 37:10-11 (KJV)* The tribe moves to Egypt to escape the famine in Canaan.

When you suffer hardship, you aren't always allowed to understand God's purpose until years later. There will be times you come out of a situation, God has blessed you to go forth, and suddenly out of nowhere, God calls your attention to the then and now. There is recognition in your spirit that enlightens you to what God has done. People may have plans for you but God has other plans. *(For I know the thoughts that I think toward you, saith the* LORD, *thoughts of peace, and not of evil, to give you an expected end.) Jer 29:11 (KJV)* Remain faithful to God in all you do. Do not compromise, especially when the vision/dream is slow in coming to pass.

REFLECTION QUESTIONS

1. Do you allow others to change the plans God has for you and push their plans for you on you? Have you done this to anyone?
2. Do you know of an experience where God worked through someone else to preserve you?
3. Is there any trial that you went through and you know specifically it was training for a particular area in your life?
4. How long after a trial was over that you were enlightened to the purpose?

PRAYER

Father, Thank You for the plans You have for me. Help me to recognize my oppositions as training and preparation to fulfill the dream. Give me wisdom and understanding. Help me to be confident to know that You are always with me. Amen.

Opposition, Opposition

By Bobbie (B J) Williams

The work is great, the need much greater.
I am a servant of the Lord God, my creator.

A great opponent you are, with plenty of skill.
I am greater than you; I choose to do God's Will.
You've opposed me time after time; I'd confess I would overcome.
You've threatened me and fought me, with God's favor I've won.

Opposition, opposition-oh I know you so well.
One thing about you: you've given me great stories to tell.
I don't take you lightly; I know you mean what you say.
In regards to your accusations and rumors, I will pray.

You've provoked me to be strong; you've taught me to be alert.
You've given me the opportunity to prevail through hurt.

I'm aware you will always be around.
I'll remain steadfast, unmovable always determined to abound.

Opposition, opposition you come again and again.
As long as I follow God's plan, I will always win.

We've fought long and we've fought hard.
No glory for me, all the glory is God's reward.

As I humbly submit at my Master's feet.
He is the author of your defeat.

My HERO

By Bobbie (BJ) Williams

Thank you for the oppositions that came my way.
Always knowing in my heart, they could not stay.

They came, pressured and prodded me, trying to set me back.
With your guidance Lord, I managed to stay on track.

Through all the rough seasons and the tears that were shed.
I could always hear your still small voice whispering: "Go ahead".

A voice so familiar, one I recognized and knew.
Saying: Lean not to my own understanding, but trust in you.

Thank you for my oppositions, they taught me to trust you and
love you more.
Thank you for my oppositions, you always rescued me, you are
MY HERO!

O h what a wonderful day it is!

P romises pending,

P rophecies to be fulfilled,

O pposition presses upon my heel.

S ufficient is God's grace for me,

I n Christ I have liberty.

T oday is essential,

I mportant work: I can no longer set aside,

O pposition awaits me to step with my every stride,

N o I can't quit, God assured me; He is on my side.

By Bobbie (BJ) Williams

I Speak

By Bobbie (B J) Williams

I speak says the Lord: From the womb you were ordained,
I speak says the Lord: Go forth, bring forth fruit, it shall remain.

I speak says the Lord: You shall walk by faith and not by sight,
I speak says the Lord: You shall walk in My power and in My might.

I speak says the Lord: I shall be your cloud by day and your pillar
of fire by night,
I speak says the Lord: I shall be your sun in the morning; I shall
be your guiding light.

I speak says the Lord: I shall strengthen you in time of need,
I speak says the Lord: You shall not stumble nor fall to your knees.

I speak says the Lord: Fear not, I am with you always, therefore stand!
I speak says the Lord: I shall give you great favor and good
understanding with man.

I speak says the Lord: You shall greatly be blessed,
I speak says the Lord: In Me you shall have great success.

Opposition gives you an opportunity to exalt God above your circumstances.

Behind every circumstance, every trial, and every opposition there is a significant reason. Your circumstance is God's opportunity.